At 12.30 p.m. Jo arrives at the airport. First she signs in at the Reception desk.

Next Jo puts her suitcase on the conveyor belt. This takes the luggage to be loaded on to the aeroplane.

3

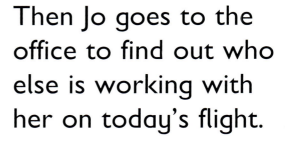

Then Jo goes to the office to find out who else is working with her on today's flight.

She looks at the computer to check how many passengers there are on the flight.

A Day in the Life of a...

Flight Attendant

Harriet Hains

W

FRANKLIN WATTS
LONDON • SYDNEY

Jo is a flight attendant. She works for Air New Zealand. Today Jo is flying from New Zealand to America. She packs her suitcase for the long journey ahead.

At 3.30 p.m. Jo and the rest of the crew
have a meeting to plan for the flight.
"The weather looks fine for take-off,"
says the Flight Superintendent.

Once she is on the plane, Jo checks the safety equipment. At 5 p.m. the passengers come on board. "Good evening," says Jo. "Your seat is just here on the right."

When everyone is on the plane
Jo explains the safety instructions.
"Is there anything you don't understand?"
she asks one lady.

"This is a long flight," Jo tells Sarah and Tom. "Would you like a fun pack each to help pass the time?" Now the children have lots of things to do.

8

It's almost time for take-off. Jo shuts the overhead lockers tightly so that nothing can fall out. She checks that the passengers have fastened their seatbelts.

Once the plane is in the air Jo prepares the meals. "I need children's meals for Sarah and Tom," she says to herself.

Next Jo checks that she has enough food and drink on her trolley for everyone in her part of the plane.

Jo serves the evening meal. "Could I have a cold beer please?" asks one of the passengers.

"Certainly, sir!" says Jo. She serves the drinks from the trolley which she pushes up and down the corridor.

Next Jo goes to the 'cockpit' at the front of the plane. This is where the pilot and co-pilot sit. They take it in turns to eat. "Would you like chicken or beef for dinner?" asks Jo.

When dinner is over, Jo clears everything away. Now she can chat to the passengers and check that they are comfortable and happy.

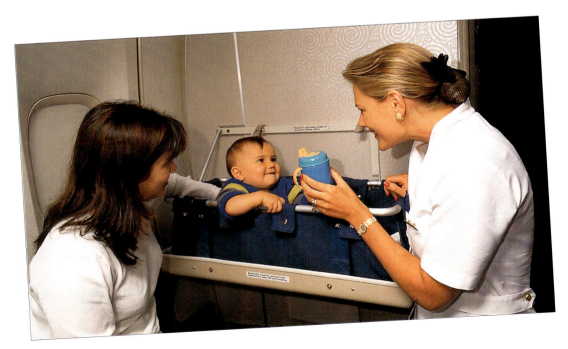

As it is a long flight, the crew members take it in turns to rest. When most of the passengers are asleep, Jo can sleep for a few hours too.

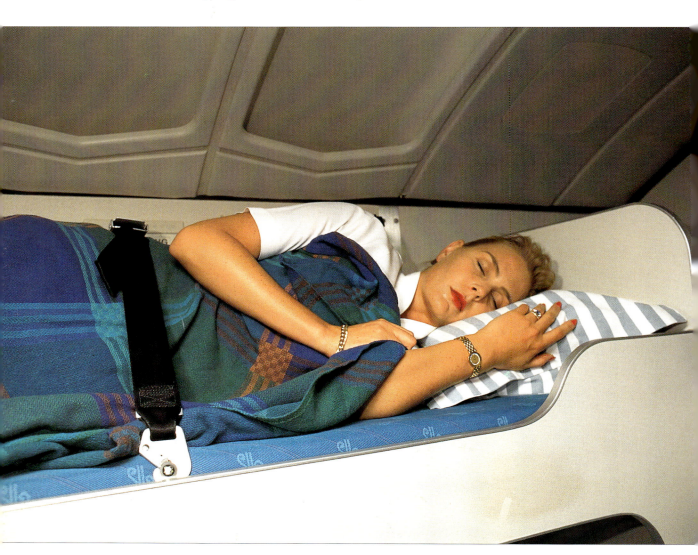

It's morning! Now it's time for Jo to serve breakfast. "We will be landing in about three hours," she tells the passengers.

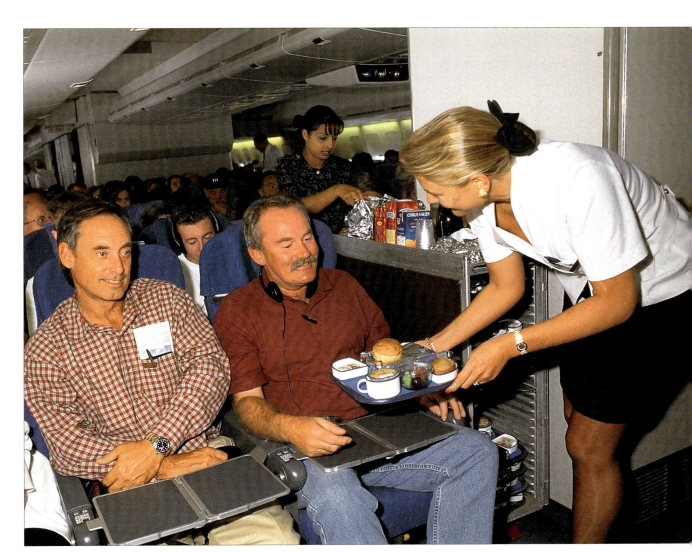

Soon it is time to get ready for landing.
Jo hands out sweets to the passengers.
Sucking sweets helps to prevent earache
as the plane comes down to land.

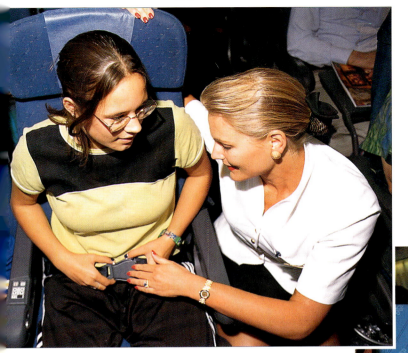

"Can you fasten
your seatbelt, please?"
Jo asks one girl.
Once all the
passengers are safely
in their seats, Jo
straps herself in, too.

It's 9.35 a.m. and at last the plane lands in America. It slowly 'taxis' to a halt. When the pilot says it is safe to do so, Jo opens the doors.

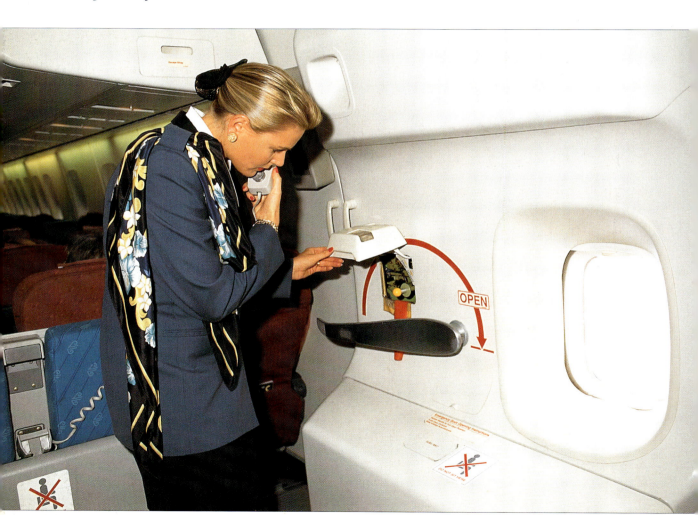

"I hope you enjoyed your flight," says Jo as she shows the passengers off the plane.

Now Jo can go to the hotel and have a long sleep. She starts the journey back to New Zealand tomorrow.

Make your own fun pack for your flight

When you go on a long flight it is a good idea to pack a small bag to keep with you on the plane. Put into the bag all the things you would like to make you comfortable and happy while you travel.

Things you may need:

1. Coloured pens, pencils and a notepad for drawing or playing games.

2. Your favourite book or comic to read.

3. A quiz book to keep you busy.

4. Some woolly socks. (Sometimes it gets cool at night on a long flight.)

5. A plastic bottle of drinking water or juice. (It is important to drink a lot on a long plane journey.)

6. A hairbrush or comb to get out the tangles at the end of your journey.

7. A toothbrush to freshen up your teeth.

Do not use computer games, radios or personal stereos on the flight as they may stop the plane's equipment from working properly.

How you can help your flight attendant

1. Find your seat quickly and sit in it until everyone else is seated too.

2. Always fasten your seatbelt when you are told to.

3. Once the plane is in the air stay in your seat and play or read quietly.

4. Remember that other passengers may be trying to sleep or watch the film so don't shout or laugh loudly.

5. If you want to use the toilet or feel sick tell an adult immediately.

6. Don't run up and down the corridors of the plane. Always walk.

7. Make sure you have all your belongings with you before you leave the plane.

Facts about flight attendants

All flight attendants are specially trained. First they go to a training course where they learn how to look after and serve passengers, what to do in an emergency and all about the aeroplane and the equipment. Then they work for 3 or 4 months on different flights. They go to another course and after that, they are fully trained.

To be a flight attendant you need to have lots of energy. Flight attendants have to lift heavy luggage and be able to stand or walk about without sitting down for a long time. They have to be tall enough to reach all the overhead equipment and, if they wear glasses or contact lenses, they have to be able to see quite well when they are not wearing them. Flight attendants need to have a friendly personality and dress smartly.

Flight attendants lead busy lives. They are often away from home for up to 2 weeks at a time and they also have to work at weekends.

Index

This edition 2003

Franklin Watts
96 Leonard Street
LondonEC2A 4XD

Franklin Watts Australia
45-51 Huntley Street
Alexandria NSW 2015

© 1998 Franklin Watts

Dewey Decimal Classification
Number: 387 7

A CIP catalogue record for
this book is available from the
British Library.

ISBN: 0 7496 4109 6

Printed in Malaysia

Editor: Samantha Armstrong
Designer: Louise Snowdon
Photographer: Chris Fairclough
Illustrations: Nick Ward

With thanks to: Jo Watson and
Air New Zealand.